If Truth Be Told

If Truth Be Told

Beverley Cooper

If Truth Be Told
first published 2016 by
Scirocco Drama
An imprint of J. Gordon Shillingford Publishing Inc.

Scirocco Drama Editor: Glenda MacFarlane
Cover design by Terry Gallagher/Doowah Design Inc.
Author photo by John Jarvis
Production photos by Terry Marzo

Printed and bound in Canada on 100% post-consumer recycled paper.

We acknowledge the financial support of the Manitoba Arts Council and The Canada Council for the Arts for our publishing program.

Suzanne DePoe
Creative Technique Inc. Artists Management
483 Euclid Ave, Toronto On. M6G 2T1
416-944-0475
email: suzanne@ctiam.ca

Library and Archives Canada Cataloguing in Publication

Cooper, Beverley, author
If truth be told / Beverley Cooper.

A play.
ISBN 978-1-927922-28-6 (paperback)

I. Title.

PS8555.O588413 2016 C812'.54 C2016-906473-5

J. Gordon Shillingford Publishing
P.O. Box 86, RPO Corydon Avenue, Winnipeg, MB Canada R3M 3S3

To my girlfriends, who support me all along the journey.

You know who you are.

Beverley Cooper

Beverley is a writer, actor and teacher. She has written for TV, film and extensively for CBC radio drama, twice being nominated for Writers Guild of Canada Awards. Plays include *Thin Ice* (co-written with Banuta Rubess, Chalmers / Dora Award, Theatre Direct plus numerous other productions), *The Eyes of Heaven* (Blyth Festival), *The Woman in White* (adapted from the novel by Wilkie Collins, Theatre Aquarius), *The Lonely Diner: Al Capone in Euphemia Township* (Blyth Festival), and *Janet Wilson Meets the Queen* (nominated for a Prix Rideaux award 2016, GCTC). *Innocence Lost: A Play about Steven Truscott* (Blyth, Centaur, National Arts Centre) was a finalist for a Governor General's Literary Award and was on the *Globe and Mail* Bestsellers List, a first for a Canadian playwright. Beverley trained as an actor at Studio 58 and has performed in TV, film and in theatres across Canada. Beverley holds an MFA in Creative Writing from the University of Guelph. She recently received a Chalmers Arts Fellowship to look at ways to renew the art of radio drama.

www.BeverleyCooper.com

Production History

If Truth Be Told premiered at The Blyth Festival July 29th, 2016.

Directed by Miles Potter

Peg .... Catherine Fitch
Maysie .... Rebecca Auerbach
Carmella................................. Anita La Selva
Jennifer .... Meghan Chalmers
Harry .... JD Nicholson
Offstage voices .... Rachel Bundy,
Nora McLellan,
Callan Potter

Set and lighting: Steve Lucas

Costume designer: Shawn Kerwin

Projections designer: Beth Kates for Playground Studios Inc.

Sound designer: Lyon Smith

If Truth Be Told was commissioned and developed by The Blyth Festival. Artistic Director, Gil Garratt.

Cast

Peg Dunlop	writer, 50
Maysie Pigot	40ish
Jennifer Pigot	18
Harry Briggs	Presbyterian Church elder and school trustee
Carmella Thorpe	school teacher, 40ish, Guatemalan, hint of Spanish accent

Offstage voices:

Iris Fowler	Peg's Mother, 70s
Kevin Briggs	18
Sharon	18

Playwright's Notes

A couple of years ago I was speaking with Randy Read, the Artistic Director of the New Stages Theatre Company. He had an idea for a play, which he gracefully passed on to me. In the 1970s and 80s there was a movement to remove "questionable" books from Ontario high school curricula, in particular books by Margaret Laurence *(The Diviners)* and Alice Munro *(Lives of Girls and Women).* Christian groups and parents in Huron County and Peterborough fought both for and against the censorship of these (and other) novels. The idea intrigued me and I began researching the story. These two brilliant writers fascinated me, their passion for writing and their complex relationships to the communities in which they lived.

While I have been writing this play, parents have been voicing both support and concerns over the proposed Ontario Sexual Education Curriculum. Their voices have helped me try to understand both sides of this story. As a parent, I know that our desire to protect our children can bring out the best and the worst of human nature.

I want to thank Deb Sholdice, Marion de Vries and Gil Garrett for championing and supporting this play; Brock Vodden, Keith Raulston, Erika Diaz and The Huron County Library for research help; Dave Carley, who is very proud of the fact that, in his hometown of Peterborough, a highly organized community response ensured that *The Diviners* and *Lives of Girls and Women* remained on school reading lists; Mary Adachi for sharing her precious files on Margaret Laurence with me; my first workshop readers, Sarah Orenstein, Sarah Dodd, Ximena Huizi, and Abigail Fernandes; and the extraordinary cast and crew in Blyth who first brought this play to life. I am always very grateful for the love and encouragement I receive from my dear ones: John, Will and Mac. Finally, I want to thank Miles Potter, who is not only one heck of a director and dramaturge but also, happily, my friend.

Catherine Fitch as Peg in the 2016 Blyth Festival production of *If Truth Be Told*.

ACT ONE

It's fall. The timeframe of the play is the 1970s, though there should be a feeling of timelessness. The set is suggestive, spare, poetic rather than realistic. There is a staircase that leads to a second floor. There is a simple oak table and chairs. There are shelves filled with books. There will be projections: perhaps images that help with the placing of the scenes. There will also be projected words.

Scene One: Wayford Town Hall / Fowler Home

Projection: "Wayford Town Hall 1977"

HARRY and CARMELLA stand before an audience of concerned parents.

HARRY: Good evening. My name is Harry Briggs. I am a school trustee with the Ellice County Board of Education and a church elder at St. Stephen's.

I am speaking today on behalf of a delegation of six: myself, my wife Laurel, our three children and God.

CARMELLA: My name is Carmella Thorpe. I am an English teacher at Wayford Secondary.

HARRY: Not only do I have a moral stake in the issue at hand, I also have a personal one: my son Kevin attends Wayford Secondary.

CARMELLA: I'm so glad to see such a big turnout tonight, so many of you joining us in our fight. I want to recognize the support of The Writers' Union of Canada, The Canadian Booksellers Association—

HARRY: Thank you all for coming, in particular the groups *based in our own community* who are working hard to rally good people around this issue, The Western Ontario Chapter of Right to Life—

CARMELLA: —The Ontario Secondary School Teachers Federation, The Freedom of Expression Committee—

HARRY: —as well as Renaissance Canada, The Committee of Citizens for Decency and Concerned Citizens for Bible Centred Religious Education in our Schools—

CARMELLA: I also want to thank the editorial staff of the *Globe and Mail* and the *Toronto Star* who have written very supportive pieces this week. And, of course, a big thanks to all of you who have come out on this rainy evening.

HARRY: I want to start by expressing my deep concerns about the kind of principles our community is passing on to our sons and daughters—

CARMELLA: This issue is not only about freedom of expression, and the kind of values we want to pass on to students: values of tolerance, empathy, openness—

HARRY: Values like respect, decency, integrity—

CARMELLA: —however this has also become a personal issue, a mean-spirited attack on one of Wayford's citizens, because a few people don't like the way she writes, the words she uses, or the stories she tells.

HARRY: This issue is, in no way, a personal attack on the writer Peg Dunlop, who obviously grew up here in Wayford.

In another area—the Fowler Home—PEG enters with a suitcase.

Projection: "One month earlier."

Projections/sound: Peg's memories. Subtle: Her father, mother, childhood voices…

CARMELLA: Reading material, what we are drawn to or moved by…is always a personal taste…but I urge you to read these novels and decide for yourself, before passing judgment on the books, or the four writers.

HARRY: I don't know if these books are good or not. I'm going to leave the judging of their literary merits to others more qualified than I.

CARMELLA: These novels represent some of the very best writing, dealing with the world we live in today.

PEG: Hello?

CARMELLA: All of the writers have written these books to great acclaim, including Peg Dunlop, and we should be very proud that she is one of our own.

HARRY: I have no issue with what these writers, including Mrs. Dunlop, write about. But I do have an issue with what material is being taught to my son.

PEG: *(PEG calls up the stairs.)* Hello?

IRIS (VO): Maysie, is that you? Is it tea?

PEG: No, Mum, it's Peg…I've come home.

Scene Two: Fowler Home

MAYSIE is laying out bills on the table. Her daughter JENNIFER is sucking on a Tootsie Pop.

JENNIFER: Why not?

MAYSIE: Because I said so.

JENNIFER: That's really helpful.

MAYSIE: You know why.

JENNIFER: It's a school trip. I have to go.

MAYSIE: You can go to a museum any time, they don't need to make you pay for a whole bus.

JENNIFER: So I'm the only one who won't be able to go?

MAYSIE: You can go if you pay for it.

JENNIFER: Can ya at least lend me some?

MAYSIE: *(Lowering her voice.)* I haven't been paid yet.

JENNIFER: Well ask her already.

MAYSIE: Shhhh!

JENNIFER: 'N I should be paid for all the times I had to—

MAYSIE: Don't start on me.

JENNIFER: I'm not starting!

MAYSIE: *(Low and terse.)* Make yourself useful. Go do those dishes.

JENNIFER leaves. PEG is coming down the stairs. MAYSIE returns to the receipts and bills on the table.

PEG: She's lost all her nouns. "Window" seems to have disappeared entirely from her vocabulary. "Can you open the..." "It's over by the..." But then she talks in minute detail about Dad picking raisins out of his carrot cake with his fork and lining them up on his plate. She remembers that but forgets the names of her grandchildren.

MAYSIE: Well, she didn't really see them all that often.

PEG: We spent three entire summers here, I spent weeks driving back and forth, six times across this GD country. We flew her and Dad out for Christmas, twice.

MAYSIE: And kids change so much.

PEG: What's this?

MAYSIE: Oh. I got everything set out here for you to look at.... Groceries, prescriptions and such. Basically what needed doing. There's bills due, end of week. That's this pile.

PEG starts to look them over.

I was just keeping an eye on things, 'cause she was making mistakes. Paying the same bill two or three times or not at all. I found all sorts of unopened bills and letters under her bed. In a shoe box.

PEG picks up a paper.

It's all on the up and up. You can check it all over.

PEG: How long have you been doing this?

MAYSIE: Few months maybe. Since early summer. One night, a Saturday, I'd been helping at the church supper and I ran into her, out in her plaid suit, going for a dentist appointment. At nine o'clock on a Saturday night. From then on, I've been keeping an eye out. Started noticing things. 'N coming more often. She wanted me to.

PEG: Why didn't you call me?

MAYSIE: She said not to. That it'd worry you. "Don't you tell Peg about my foolishness, nothing she can do..."

PEG: Well, there's certainly nothing I can do if I don't know what is going on.

MAYSIE: She's been downhill since your dad. And this doesn't help of course. She's really worse since.

PEG: Yes, now she's strapped in up there, like a lunatic.

MAYSIE: She was forgetting she was hurt and hopping up. Broken ankle at her age takes time.

PEG: Yes, I know.

MAYSIE: I've been moving her round so she don't get bedsores. And trying to keep up the food. She'd been eating like a bird. There was nothing in the cupboards but beans.

PEG: I wish someone had told me.

MAYSIE: Well.... You were awful far away.

So, I've got it all listed here. Groceries I bought and whatnot.

PEG tries to take it all in. JENNIFER appears.

JENNIFER: Mum.

MAYSIE: You remember Jennifer?

JENNIFER: Hi.

PEG: Jennifer. Goodness. Look at you.... Children really are concrete time, aren't they?

MAYSIE: She's been a big help here.

PEG: Right, you've got three.

MAYSIE: Two. Alistair's fourteen.

JENNIFER: Mr. Briggs is at the back door.

MAYSIE: Oh yeah, tell him to come in.

JENNIFER leaves.

PEG: Who?

MAYSIE: Harry Briggs from church. Elder Briggs.

PEG: What does he want? As if Mum hasn't given enough to that church.

MAYSIE: No, I forgot to tell ya, he's—

HARRY enters in his coat, holding a casserole. JENNIFER comes in behind him.

HARRY: I'm not staying. I just wanted to say welcome back, Peg. Laurel has made you a casserole.

PEG: That's very kind.

HARRY: How's the patient?

PEG: I had no idea she'd gone downhill so badly.

HARRY: She wasn't really that bad, till she fell.

He hands the casserole to JENNIFER, who takes it into the kitchen before she returns.

MAYSIE: Harry's been checking in on Mrs. Fowler regular. Sittin' with her.

HARRY: Some from the Ladies' Auxiliary have been by as well. Of course it's been mostly Maysie here, she's a wonder woman.

PEG: Yes, Doctor Addison told me.

HARRY: She's the one who found Iris. You tell her?

MAYSIE: She was right there. Bottom of the stairs. In a heap. Whimpering. Don't know how long she'd been there. Been trying to carry a box of apples to the attic. I don't know where she got that idea.

HARRY: Lucky you found her at all.

MAYSIE: Wasn't one of my regular days. I do Bernhardt's on Wednesdays. But on a nice day Mrs. Fowler's always out front with her coffee. So I had a feeling. As I say, I've been keeping an eye out more.

JENNIFER: Mum… I gotta go do homework.

MAYSIE: OK. You go. I won't be long. Turn the water on for the noodles. 'N make sure Alistair's done what he needs before his soccer.

JENNIFER: *(Leaving.)* 'Kay.

HARRY: How long you here for, Peg?

PEG: I guess I'm in for the long haul now. Seems she can't be left alone anymore. So as long as she needs me, I guess.

HARRY: Ohh, that'll be good for Iris. She'll like having you back. And your mister, Ted isn't it? …he coming too?

PEG: No. He's staying in Vancouver.

HARRY: Ahh…Well, I'd better be on my way. Don't be a stranger. Come on Sunday. Reverend Clarke is there now. He gives a good sermon.

PEG: Thank Laurel for me, for the casserole.

HARRY: Will do. Congratulations on all your success, Peg. And welcome back to Wayford.

HARRY leaves.

PEG: Seems like I'm the last to know about the condition my mother was in. Lord help me, I never thought I'd be living back in this town, everyone knowing my business.

MAYSIE: You'll need to taste that first.

Pause.

MAYSIE: The casserole. I was in Home Ec with Laurel.

There is an awkward pause.

I was kinda hoping we could square things up today.

PEG: Of course. Let me find my chequebook.

PEG digs in her purse for her chequebook.

You can stay on, Maysie, right? I can't manage this all on my own. I've got to have time to write.

MAYSIE: I suppose I could. I got my regular houses I gotta keep going, though.

PEG: I can be somewhat flexible about times.

MAYSIE: Jennifer might be interested in making a little extra money as well. If I can't be here.

PEG: I've got a deadline, so I'll have to keep at it. I'll need to take ownership of this table.

She looks at all the papers on the table. MAYSIE gets her coat on and waits.

Do you mind if we settle this tomorrow? I can't think straight at the moment.

PEG starts picking up all the papers.

MAYSIE: OK….

See you in the morning then… Yeah, if I could get a cheque first thing…. I've got banking that needs done.

PEG: Of course.

MAYSIE leaves. PEG puts the bills etc. in a drawer in the table. She takes out a pad of paper out and a pen. She lights a cigarette, thinking.

Scene Three: Fowler Home

PEG is writing at the table. CARMELLA stands with her coat on, mid-speech.

CARMELLA: I just think your book—*The Women of Time*—is the most beautiful, complicated—

PEG makes a gesture for her to move it along.

Anyway, I'm teaching the Grade Twelve and Thirteen English classes at the high school and *Women of Time* is on the reading list this year and we are about to start that unit next week and so I wonder if you'd be able to come in and speak to two of the classes. They'd be so thrilled. I mean, the fact that you are from this very town and that you are writing about the kind of people they know—

PEG puts her hand up.

PEG: I'm going to make this simple for you and just say "no." If I said yes to every request I received—for interviews, book endorsements, speaking engagements and so on—I'd never get a lick of work done. I do my bit when my books come out but then I have to protect my writing time. I've had to come back to care for my mother, so I've got enough on my plate...Thank you for asking, but I'm going to say no.

PEG stands up. She puts out her hand.

Nice to meet you...sorry, I've forgotten...

CARMELLA: Carmella Thorpe. I'm married to Leonard. He says hello, actually.

PEG: Little Lennie Thorpe? He was just learning to pick his nose last I saw him. I looked after him when his mum was in the hospital with her second.

CARMELLA: Yes, I know.

PEG: So you must be the one from Guatemala.

CARMELLA: Yes.

PEG: Your English is very good.

CARMELLA: My mother was American. We spoke English at home.

PEG: I remember when Lennie was down there working for the Mennonite church. Seemed so exotic. Must be quite the change for you, moving here.

CARMELLA: Yes.

PEG: How do you like the winters?

CARMELLA: Ohhh—

PEG: And the folks of Wayford, have they welcomed you with open arms?

CARMELLA: It takes a little time to get to know people but—

PEG: I was practically run out of this town for wanting to be a writer. That just wasn't done. I was supposed to be making casseroles, cleaning house, preserving jams.

CARMELLA: It hasn't been—

PEG: But you really are from away. I don't suppose that's easy.

CARMELLA: No but…I do like it here. The landscape is so beautiful.

PEG: I couldn't wait to get out of here. And now I'm back. Glutton for punishment.

CARMELLA: No, no, it's not that bad, really. Many people have been very kind. It's just that…

PEG: Yes?

CARMELLA: I'm aware I'm an outsider. That's all. I'm hoping that will change.

PEG: Sure, sure… that will change. In about fifty years.

Pause.

I'll come speak to your class, Mrs. Thorpe. Give me a call next week and we'll set it up.

CARMELLA: Really? You sure?

PEG: I just said I would.

CARMELLA: Yes, I'll call you Monday morning, first thing.

PEG: Call me in the afternoon. I don't answer the phone in the mornings.

CARMELLA: The students are going to be so excited to meet you.

Scene Four: School Classroom

PEG sits on a chair, facing out at a sea of students. She has a copy of The Women of Time *on her lap. CARMELLA stands beside her.*

CARMELLA: Does no one have a question for our guest? A world-famous writer? Books sold in many countries?

PEG: Seventeen languages actually.

CARMELLA: Seventeen!

PEG: I'm not actually famous. Just with librarians and bookworms. And they're an odd lot, really.

CARMELLA: Students?

Silence. PEG nervously takes a cigarette out. She's about to light it, thinks better of it, puts it away.

Perhaps you'd like to ask Mrs. Dunlop a question about winning the Governor General's Award, one of the most prestigious awards a writer can receive in Canada.

Silence.

We will all be reading her book, starting next week. So perhaps you want to get a head start, ask about themes, symbols, metaphoric imagery...topics we've been learning about?

PEG: Metaphoric imagery! Even I don't know the answer to that one.

Sound: a couple of titters.

CARMELLA: Perhaps a question about writing methods.... outlines... character development...

Silence.

All right, I have a question. Where do you get your ideas from?

PEG: Oh dear. There is a danger, I always think, in speaking about creativity, analyzing too much.

Pause.

But...In some ways it's about work ethic. Sitting down every day and writing, not questioning if it's really good or not, just getting things down on paper and then reworking it, finding rhythms, pulling it apart and putting it back together.

CARMELLA: You see, students, just what I've said about writing being rewriting.

PEG: But where the ideas come from...that's more complex. Sometimes someone tells you something unusual that sparks a story, or it's a memory, a bit of childhood I want to explore a bit, or I see a woman on the street, you know, very well dressed, and she looks desperately unhappy and I begin to imagine her life. Trying to get at the nub. And.... well, inspiration can be all those things. Sometimes an idea comes from unexpected places. Oh! Like Marion Flowerdew.

Sound: a couple of titters.

Some years ago, in Vancouver, at my son's high school, parents were trying to raise money for the library. People were donating various items to be auctioned off. Tickets to football games and so on. I'd had four books published by then, and one of the mums suggested that we auction off someone being written into one of my books; the right for the successful bidder's name to be the name of a character. I thought that was fine. I could use any name, really, for the right incidental character. A woman from the British Properties area paid over four hundred dollars for that. Her name was Marion Flowerdew. And I loved the name, imagined her as a character, and, of course, she eventually became the older woman living on the farm in *The Women of Time*.

Right. They actually haven't read it yet.

CARMELLA: Oh, that's a lovely story. Where one finds inspiration! So interesting. All right, students, back to you. Remember participation is part of your mark.

Silence.

Kevin! Good. You've got a question. Please stand up. Now go ahead.

KEVIN (VO): That prize you got—

CARMELLA: The Governor General's Award for Literature.... Yes?

KEVIN (VO): What did you get? A trophy or?

PEG: It was a monetary prize.

KEVIN (VO): You mean you got money? How much?

PEG: $5000.

KEVIN (VO): Geez. Wow. What did you have to do to get that?

PEG: Write every day for about two years. Wait for it to be edited. Write for another year. More edits. More rewrites. Have it be published. Have it be judged by my peers. Win. Travel to Ottawa.

KEVIN (VO): And do you make other money from writing?

PEG: Yes, I do. I get a portion, a very small portion, of every book that is sold, so if my book sells well, then I make a living and if it doesn't do well, I don't.

KEVIN (VO): So is writing your job?

PEG: Yes.

KEVIN (VO): But not like a real job, working in a factory or on a farm or teaching or something.

PEG: I think of it as a real job.

KEVIN (VO): I mean, isn't it more like a hobby? So my mother makes cakes and sells them to folks but I wouldn't call that—

PEG: No it's not a hobby. I am a writer. I have devoted the past thirty years of my life, writing, every day.

KEVIN (VO): But what happens if you don't sell enough books? What does your husband do?

PEG: If I don't sell enough books then I am in financial trouble. I do not depend on a husband for my income.

CARMELLA: All right. I think we all know that writing is most certainly a job, possibly with some uncertainty, but I'm sure Mrs. Dunlop doesn't have to worry about her books selling well. Oh Sharon, good girl, you've got your hand up. What's your question? Stand up now.

SHARON (VO): My mother says your husband has divorced you because you wrote about him in one of your books. Is that true?

Sound: Classroom titters.

CARMELLA: That's not an appropriate question, Sharon. Sit down. We will speak about that after class. Everyone, focus! Eyes up here. I'm going to ask Mrs. Dunlop to read a selection from her book. I want you all to sit up respectfully and give her your full attention. Any further rudeness will be dealt with during a detention.

PEG opens her copy of The Women of Time. *She goes to a marked selection and begins to read.*

PEG: "Marion Flowerdew arose at 7:06, like she did every single morning, timing her awakening so she didn't have to listen to the horrors of the news when the clock radio went off."

PEG voice continues to read as music comes up.

Projection/Sound: The words are projected across the stage, floating and soaring across the walls: "The one-eyed cat took this as his cue to jump on the bed, landing directly on her soft abdomen, momentarily leaving her breathless. Marion batted the cat aside and sat up, opening her dry eyes to the morning world. She placed her stiffened feet on the cold oak flooring, and stood up, trying to arrange her bones in the correct order, then made her way to the washroom, where, once again, the pipes had frozen."

Scene Five: Fowler Home

PEG lights a cigarette, looking out the window, thinking, thinking. After a moment JENNIFER comes down the stairs carrying a mug.

JENNIFER: She doesn't want a mug. She wants a real teacup.

She disappears in the kitchen for a moment. PEG sits and begins to write. JENNIFER returns.

Did somebody move the sugar?

PEG: *(Not looking up.)* Cupboard to the left.

JENNIFER: I looked there.

PEG: Try above the stove.

JENNIFER leaves. There is some banging in the kitchen before she returns with a teacup and takes it upstairs.

JENNIFER: *(Off.)* Here you go.

JENNIFER returns. PEG does not acknowledge her.

You writing another book?

PEG: Trying to.

JENNIFER: I was in the class you came to talk to the other day.

PEG: Mmm?

JENNIFER: Yeah.

PEG: Everyone was very stimulated by my presence. I could tell.

JENNIFER: Why were you nervous?

PEG: Was I?

JENNIFER: Yeah. Ya looked nervous.

PEG: I don't like talking about my work.

JENNIFER: Why'd you read that part about the old lady?

PEG: Where's your mother today?

JENNIFER: Taking my brother to the doctor's. Why didn't you read from the beginning with the teenage girl and the boy from town?

PEG: You've read it?

JENNIFER: Started. I'm a slow reader, so Mrs. Thorpe let me have it early. I hate reading mostly.

PEG: The beginning of the book is more complex, it has a certain rhythm that needs time to develop—What's wrong with your brother?

JENNIFER: He has a weird rash on his hands and feet and in his throat. He can't swallow.

PEG: Hand, Foot and Mouth disease. My daughter had that twice. Ghastly.

JENNIFER: You have kids?

PEG: Two. All grown up. What's your father do? Is he the type of father who could take his son to the doctor or does he think that is women's work?

JENNIFER: Dad doesn't live with us. He works up north, fixing boats and stuff. I never see him.

Pause.

They're divorced.

PEG: When did that happen?

JENNIFER: You're divorced too, right?

PEG: No. But yes, probably...eventually. If either of us has enough energy to go through with all the paperwork.

JENNIFER: I heard two ladies in the Woolworths the other day. I work there Saturdays. Talking about you, and your husband not coming.

PEG: Oh that's nice. Lovely to know.

PEG returns to her work. After a moment:

JENNIFER: Dad left back when my kid brother died.

PEG turns her attention back to Jennifer.

PEG: Your…brother?

JENNIFER: Yeah. Finn.

PEG: I had no idea.

JENNIFER: He drowned.

PEG: Oh, that's terrible.

How old was he?

JENNIFER: Two, almost three. He was really cute. He would eat cookies with his feet. Picked up cookies with his toes and ate them, for no reason. His hands worked perfect.

PEG: Was it…a boating accident?

JENNIFER: No…we was camping in Georgian Bay with another family with kids. And it was hot and we were swimming. 'N there was a big rock with a diving board on it, really high above the water. We were jumping off the high dive board and Mum was watching Finn and that was OK. And then it was getting dark and we had to get out and were drying by the bonfire. And Dad was kinda throwing Finnie around, like goofin' around and Mum was worrying about the fire. So Finn wasn't allowed to goof around anymore. But then he'd get close again to get Dad to pull him off. A sorta game thing. And Dad started to get mad at him, so Mum said she'd toast Finn a marshmallow, and he wanted to toast it himself, of course, and burnt it, so Mum had to toast him another one. And when she turned to give Finn his marshmallow…he was standing at the end of the diving board. Maybe ten feet above the water. Everybody just stood super still. Mum talked real soft. "Finnie, come down now, OK Sweetie?" And he jumped.

PEG: My god…

JENNIFER: The water was pitch black. Dad dove in and everyone shone their flashlights but he'd sunk right outta sight.

PEG: ….I can't imagine.

JENNIFER: They didn't find him for three days. They didn't want me to see him. But I did.

PEG: You poor thing…Your poor mother.

JENNIFER: She was wrecked. The minister had to come talk to her every day for about a month before she'd get out of bed. Don't tell her I told you. She does not like to talk about it.

PEG: I won't. No. I'm so sorry.

JENNIFER: Dad left us right after.

PEG: A terrible accident.

JENNIFER: Yeah.

Long pause.

PEG: I think I'll go for a walk. You OK to stay till I get back?

JENNIFER: Yeah…Don'tcha have to keep writing?

PEG: My writing is at an impasse.

PEG gets her coat.

You sure you're OK?

JENNIFER: Yeah.

PEG leaves. JENNIFER looks at Peg's desk. She sits in PEG's chair. Picks up a copy of The Women of Time *and reads:*

"Lissa was now fourteen years old, watching the smoothness and perfectness of the adults around her melting away to reveal selfish intentions and lies."

JENNIFER's reading voice continues with:

Projection/sound: "Her parents were not like Alphie's parents, with their green velvet sofa and creamy white carpets. Alphie's parents pronounced every syllable of a word, each letter a ripe strawberry ready to be savored. Her own parents carelessly dropped consonants like they were littering used tissues."

Scene Six: School Classroom

MAYSIE: I wanted to talk about that book by Peg Dunlop.

CARMELLA: *The Women of Time*?

MAYSIE: Yeah. Jennifer's been reading it.

CARMELLA: Yes, it's our selection for Canadian Literature.

MAYSIE takes it out of her purse.

Did Jennifer tell you that Mrs. Dunlop came and spoke to our class? It was quite something. I don't think the students quite knew what to make of it all. Such a new experience for them. To think of writing as a profession—

MAYSIE: Yeah, the thing is, I don't think this book should be read by kids.

CARMELLA: It's not being read by kids. It's assigned only to the Grade Twelve and Thirteens. Have you read the book, Mrs. Pigot?

MAYSIE: Yes I have. I stayed up all last night reading it. And I did not like it one bit.

CARMELLA: What is it about the book you don't like?

MAYSIE: The way they speak.

CARMELLA: The swearing? Authors must use authentic language or we won't believe the characters are true. I don't believe Peg Dunlop is condoning the language. But we both know people who speak like that in real life—

MAYSIE: And the way they behave.

CARMELLA: Can you give me an example?

MAYSIE: The teenagers in the first part. They do bad things and get away with it. Scot-free.

CARMELLA: What are you referring to, exactly?

MAYSIE: Sneaking around. Lying to their parents. And that other stuff.

CARMELLA: What do you think should happen?

MAYSIE: She should get pregnant or get VD. That's what happens in "real life."

CARMELLA: Not always.

MAYSIE: Or at least feel guilty. And the grandmother? A sixty-five-year-old woman and a total stranger. 'N Peg Dunlop describes it all.

CARMELLA: Oh, but it's so tastefully done. I think if you read it again, you'd see that we imagine much more than she describes. And I would say that the parts of the book that are sexual in nature really take up a few pages in a book that is over two hundred and—

MAYSIE: The husband and wife in the middle part. You telling me that's all OK?

CARMELLA: …?

MAYSIE: They can't stand each other. He's a drunk and a cheat. That's a nice view of marriage.

CARMELLA: But don't you find it so tragic? Barb and Joe get married so young, with such hope, he's so handsome, she's so pretty, but they're a bad match, which happens so often—

MAYSIE: *(Low.)* I know that couple, right? I know who she's writing about and she should not be writing about them. That's their business, not hers.

CARMELLA: But writers often draw from life experiences—

MAYSIE: She's writing about Wayford. There's a Woolworths and yellow church and a radio station—

CARMELLA: I think it's a loving tribute to a place, very much like Wayford. But it could be so many places. And I think it's so important for the students to read about the type of people they know.

MAYSIE: I don't want Jenny getting to know those type of people. They're not teaching her anything good.

CARMELLA: Reading Dickens or the works of Shakespeare is, of course, very important, but to read about the place you live, that is an unusual opportunity. It's as if they are reading a poem by Wordsworth, standing in a field of daffodils in the Lake District.

MAYSIE: We are not talking about daffodils here. I can't think of one good person in the whole book.

CARMELLA: You know this book has been critically acclaimed, translated into seventeen languages, has won the Governor General's Award for Literature?

MAYSIE: Oh, I know all about the fancy award and, actually, I don't care if it's been recommended by the Queen Mother herself…I'm not saying folks shouldn't be able to read it. I'm saying it's not fit for teaching in a high school.

CARMELLA: You know. Sometimes we like to think of our children as…well… children. When in fact, they are young adults. The students in Jennifer's class are old enough to quit school, get married, vote, join the army. They are much more sophisticated than we would like to believe. I think this book could yield some really useful conversations at home.

MAYSIE: You don't have kids, do you?

CARMELLA: No…I don't.

MAYSIE: Then don't tell me how to raise mine.

Pause.

CARMELLA: All right. I understand. Well, hopefully you'll let me do my job as a teacher. I will keep your concerns in mind and make sure the students read the book with certain caveats.

MAYSIE: So you're still going to teach it?

CARMELLA: I plan my year very carefully. The book was approved last May by the English Department. I handed out copies to all the students today. Jennifer received her copy early, so that she could get a head start.

MAYSIE: Well, she isn't going to be reading this crap.

MAYSIE puts the book in her purse.

CARMELLA: It is your right, as a parent, to raise concerns, and if you would rather I assign an another book for Jennifer to read, that is your decision, but I am afraid—

MAYSIE: Am I the first parent to talk to you?

CARMELLA: Yes, you are.

MAYSIE: Well, I betcha I won't be the last.

Scene Seven: Home of Harry Briggs

MAYSIE: She blew me off, Harry, treated me like I was one of her students, shoved in a corner with a dunce cap.

HARRY: Well, perhaps it's a cultural thing. Maybe she didn't understand fully—

MAYSIE: Oh, she understood all right. She just didn't want to hear what I was saying.

HARRY: I think she's a good teacher. Kevin seems to—

MAYSIE: Why on earth they pick a book like that? I mean, Peg Dunlop can write whatever the heck she wants, but I should have a say if my own daughter should read it. And working for her puts me in an awkward position.

Pause.

HARRY: How's Iris doing?

MAYSIE: Oh, she's still sleeping a lot. Doesn't really seem to understand that Peg's moved back. Keeps asking where's Peg's husband. Peg doesn't have much patience for that.

HARRY: I don't think patience is one of Peg's virtues.

MAYSIE: She's certainly not too happy to be back in Wayford.

HARRY: Well...I'm sure that it's tough, seeing her mother like that, and if her marriage is in some trouble—

MAYSIE: She could be more charitable though. When you dropped over Laurel's casserole, she made some comment about you coming by to get Iris's money.

HARRY: Where would she get that idea?

MAYSIE: You know how she is. Feels bad done by.

HARRY: She does seem to have some kind of grudge against Wayford. I heard her talk on the radio once, speaking about her first book, which called the town something else, but of course it's Wayford—

MAYSIE: Yep.

HARRY: She makes out like she grew up in some slum, with prostitutes and bootleggers.

MAYSIE: I'm sure the couple she writes about in her book is Janet and Steve Irwin. Right down to the way they look. You remember what he did to her. 'N the names he called her. That's all in there. Peg must have been takin' notes last time she was here.

HARRY: I don't think she was very popular as a young girl and that's shaped her in some way.

MAYSIE: Her own mother isn't happy about the books either. She told me once that she read one and didn't like it one bit.

HARRY: Lots of people do like her books.

MAYSIE: Maybe they like reading smut.

HARRY: It can't be that bad.

MAYSIE: Wait till you read it.

HARRY: Well, I'll certainly ask Kevin about it.

MAYSIE: I thought you could bring it up with the other trustees or something.

HARRY: Well, I have to read it first before taking further steps. How is Jennifer, otherwise?

MAYSIE: Fine enough. You won't be liking the language Peg Dunlop uses.

HARRY: What kind of language?

MAYSIE: Oh yes, lots of language. GD this and GD that. And…*(Low.)* A man touches himself.

HARRY: In a school book?

MAYSIE: I'm not crazy.

HARRY: That doesn't sound appropriate.

MAYSIE: That's what I'm saying. And it's not just me, the gals at the Ladies' Auxiliary was talking about it when it come out. They were having quite the chinwag.

HARRY: All right. All right. Let's not get too worked up here. First step is I need to read it and if there is anything wrong I can bring concerns forward with the other trustees-

MAYSIE: Nothing against Peg Dunlop, she's a nice enough lady—

HARRY: She is. And we need to think about Iris—

MAYSIE: Harry, you can't let anyone know it's me that's brought it up.

HARRY: All right.

MAYSIE: I need the money, working for her. Promise me, you won't.

HARRY: Of course.

MAYSIE leaves. HARRY opens the book and flips through it.

Projected words: "bodies, entwined, skin, touch, mouths, enters, hard, presses, soft, gentle, moan."

Scene Eight: Fowler Home

CARMELLA: They want to stop your book.

PEG: Stop me writing?

CARMELLA: No, no. Some parents have complained about *The Women of Time.*

PEG: Which parents?

CARMELLA: Oh, I can't say who, it's against board policy for me to—

PEG: What in heaven's name are they complaining about?

CARMELLA: The language. The swearing.

PEG: Oh, come on. I'm sure those students have heard much worse.

CARMELLA: And the teenage sex.

PEG: What? Do they think that teenagers don't think about sex? They only think about sex. Their bodies want them to think about sex. You know it's the same people who get worked up like this who don't believe in sex education, who are always anti-abortion under any circumstances—

CARMELLA: It's the last section as well.

PEG: Oh, they don't like it that a woman has consensual sex?

CARMELLA: With a stranger.

PEG: Which is worse? That she has sex with a stranger or that she has sex at age sixty-five? God, I hope I am having sex at sixty-five. I don't care who it's with. And sex has to be an aspect of a fully rounded character, surely they see that?

CARMELLA: I tried to make it clear that it makes up a miniscule part of the book.

PEG: Have they even read it?

CARMELLA: Some have, not all, I think. One parent was particularly misinformed. She thought we were teaching the Grade Nines about masturbation.

PEG: How many complaints have you got?

CARMELLA: The principal's had three phone calls, and I've had several parents come to my classroom.

PEG: What?

CARMELLA: I told them that the book had been approved by the Board of Education. That it is considered a Canadian classic…

PEG: I don't like this... Did you hear about Peterborough? Some churchy types got all whipped up about one of Margaret Laurence's novels. Practically burned her at the stake. I don't think they are through with her yet. Crazy fundamentalists. Half of them don't even believe in evolution; they want their kids to learn about Adam and Eve, but only with the fig leaves.

CARMELLA: No, no, no, it's not going to go that far; these are reasonable people. Really, Mrs. Dunlop. Please don't worry.

PEG: Are you going to stop teaching it?

CARMELLA: No, no! Of course not. I grew up in Guatemala, I do not take censorship lightly…so you see…you are in good hands. It's just a few people. And so many people here love your work. Truly.

PEG: I don't know. This town...

CARMELLA: You should just concentrate on writing your next beautiful novel.

PEG: Oh, Carmella... the sight of the empty page is a very cruel view.

CARMELLA: I'm sure you'll get one of your creative inspirations.

PEG: Hmmpt. Coleridge called writing an indescribable terror and some days I agree with him. He didn't write a poem worth reading after he was twenty-five. We must never take words for granted, Carmella. Never.

Scene Nine: Fowler Home

JENNIFER stands facing her mother. She has her coat on, her school bag over her shoulder. She holds out a book by Susanna Moodie.

JENNIFER: Look at this. I'm so embarrassed!

MAYSIE: Keep your voice down.

JENNIFER: Now I have to read some book about a stupid pioneer woman and everyone else is going to be reading *Women of Time,* which I was liking, by the way.

MAYSIE: You didn't read all of it. You don't know what it was like.

There is a knock at the door. MAYSIE goes to get it. It's HARRY.

HARRY: Is she home?

MAYSIE: She's upstairs with Mrs. Fowler.

PEG: *(Off.)* Who is it?

MAYSIE: It's Harry Briggs.

HARRY: *(Calling up to PEG.)* Can I come up?

PEG: *(Off.)* Sure, just for a minute. She's just settling.

JENNIFER: Hi, Mr. Briggs.

HARRY: How's my son behaving himself these days?

JENNIFER: OK.

HARRY starts to go up, MAYSIE grabs him by his arm.

MAYSIE: Harry.

He acknowledges her meaning and then goes up.

JENNIFER: What's going on?

MAYSIE: Nothing's going on.

JENNIFER: What's he here for?

MAYSIE takes a step or two up the stairs. Listening.

Does she know you complained?

MAYSIE: No! *(Low.)* She can't know. Don't you be telling her.

JENNIFER: Why not?

MAYSIE: *(Low.)* You want me to lose my job here, the one that's putting food in your mouth? Or would you rather write your father and ask him for a bit of help once in—

JENNIFER: OK!

MAYSIE: *(Low.)* That book is not proper reading for youths.

JENNIFER: Don't you start a big deal.

MAYSIE: I'm not going to start a big deal.

JENNIFER: Promise?

PEG and HARRY are coming down the stairs.

MAYSIE: Go and do your homework—you're babysitting at Smith's tonight.

JENNIFER: I know.

MAYSIE: You and Alistair are on your own for dinner. There's mac and cheese on the counter.

JENNIFER: All right.

JENNIFER leaves.

HARRY: Iris looks much better to me. She'll be up making pies in no time.

PEG: I think her pie-making days may be done.

HARRY: At least the straps are off.

MAYSIE: She remembers her ankle is broke now. That's something.

HARRY: If you need any help. Maybe if she's up to getting out to church?… We certainly miss her.

Pause.

I have another purpose in dropping by today, Peg.

PEG: Sounds a little ominous…Come to see if you can save my soul?

HARRY: I'm sure your soul doesn't need saving. And I'm not here to solicit a donation. So you can hang on to your wallet as well.

MAYSIE: Tea? Should I put the kettle on?

HARRY: Sure.

MAYSIE: Milk and sugar, Harry?

HARRY: Please.

MAYSIE goes into the kitchen.

How're you finding being back in Wayford?

PEG: I never thought I'd come back to live, but life takes us down unforeseen paths, so here I am.

HARRY: You don't write very favourably about Wayford.

PEG: Actually, that's not true. I'm writing about life, both good and bad, aiming for truth, for authenticity. This is the place I know, but there are complicated stories everywhere.

People here get all worked up because they think I'm writing about them, but you know, I get letters from places like Australia and they think I'm writing about their lives.

HARRY: I want to speak about your book, *The Women of Time*.

PEG: Ahhh...so that's what this is about.

HARRY: Now hear me out...There have been some concerns raised about the suitability of the book being taught in high schools.

PEG: Raised by whom?

HARRY: Parents. And some of our parishioners at St. Stephen's.

PEG: And?

HARRY: Personally, I do not deny its literary merits. I know that folks far more schooled than me, have endowed your book with many, many accolades. But I do oppose it being used as teaching material.

PEG: Surprise, surprise.

HARRY: I just feel that, in a classroom setting, where students come from a variety of circumstances, parents with various moral standards, that we should be cautious about introducing books that contravene some of those morals.

PEG: Ah, and just what morals am I contravening?

HARRY: Language that takes the Lord's name in vain. Language that is profane, blasphemous.

PEG: Have you spent any time out in the world, Harry? I can't have characters just saying "gosh golly" or "gull darn it"—

HARRY: That's not what I'm saying, Peg. I am not telling you what to write.

PEG: What are you saying?

HARRY: I'm saying it would be better if the teachers taught the classic books, ones that don't get everyone all riled up: Conrad, Dickens, Melville, books that teach great literature without offending. Perhaps we should be following St. Peter's admonition to study only what is good, wise, just and virtuous, leave other material for those who seek it out.

PEG: Yeah, perhaps they should just stick with Dick and Jane and their little dog Spot.

MAYSIE comes in with a tray holding sugar, milk, two spoons, a saucer and two mugs with teabags and hot water in them. She sets it on the table.

MAYSIE: Here we go.

HARRY: Thank you, Maysie.

IRIS (VO): Maysie! I need to get up! Who's there? Maysie!

MAYSIE: Coming, Mrs. Fowler!

MAYSIE goes upstairs. They scoop their tea bags out of the mugs onto the saucer and help themselves to milk and sugar.

HARRY: The relationships in your book are…well, I think some students would be made uncomfortable by reading some of the…

PEG: Sex, Harry? You saying you don't like the sex? .... These students are bright. They are curious. They want to know about the world. I read all kinds of books as a kid. And you know what? Reading made life feel important.

HARRY: A mother called me in tears yesterday, saying her son is being taught pornography. Now, I, for one, would not go that far, but you see how emotional people get when it comes to their children. We don't want these arguments being played out in the classroom. Let the students read your book when they are adults, once they able to make their own decisions.

PEG: Listen, I didn't put my novel on the reading list. Others did. So I don't know why the hell you are coming and crying to me about it, because a few misguided people are complaining.

HARRY: What do you mean by misguided?

PEG: Being guided by religious beliefs. A few people shouldn't be able to tell everybody else what to do.

HARRY: Aren't you imposing your own set of values with this book?

PEG: This is ridiculous. Why should I have to defend my book to you? You're not my pastor or my friend—

HARRY: Peg! I'm sorry I've upset you—

PEG: Maybe I should take Mum, move out of town, is that what you want?

HARRY: You are being unreasonable now—

PEG: Why in Christ's name did I come back here??

HARRY: Excuse me!

PEG: Well, I don't know what you want of me!

HARRY: OK, OK. I'm sorry, I've gone about this the wrong way. I just want you to be prepared, to know this is, in no way, a personal attack.

PEG: What isn't?

HARRY: Your novel is being removed from the classrooms.

PEG: What?

HARRY: Students have been asked to return their books until it can be reviewed—

PEG: The church is doing this? What authority do they—

HARRY: I'm a school trustee, Peg, not just a church elder. I thought you knew that.

PEG: No I didn't.

HARRY: My son Kevin is in that class. So, in fact, I have a vested interest as well…The superintendent has referred the matter to the Textbook Review Committee.

PEG: Textbook Review Committee? What is that?

HARRY: The board set up the TRC to review books that are questionable.

PEG: This is Orwellian. Are you banning my book? What other books are you throwing on the pyre?

HARRY: No books have been banned. But, yes, questions have been raised about other books. And it's not just here, you may have heard of concerns that parents have raised in Peterborough about a book called *The Diviners*.

PEG: Oh yes, I've heard about how Margaret Laurence has been vilified—calling her a Disciple of Satan. *The Diviners* indeed.. One of the greatest novels ever written. At least I know I'm in good company. I think you should go now, Harry.

HARRY: Fine, I just wanted to—

PEG: And by the way, I am going to be checking on all the donations my mother has made to St. Stephen's and make sure that you haven't been coercing money from a woman who is clearly—

HARRY: Peg, stop it. Don't be childish. Any donations Iris has made have been given with her good Christian heart.

PEG: Something I didn't inherit, apparently.

HARRY goes to leave.

HARRY: I wish you wouldn't take it all so personally.

PEG: When you attack my writing, you are attacking me.

HARRY: Don't shoot the messenger, Peg.

HARRY leaves. PEG looks for her cigarettes. MAYSIE comes downstairs, gathering up the tea things.

PEG: Did you hear all that nonsense?

MAYSIE: He was talking about your book, was he? Taking it out of the school? Well maybe that's for the best, not stir things up too much.

PEG: Ohh, it's too late for that. They're coming after us, Maysie.

Scene Ten: Home of Harry Briggs

HARRY enters, followed by CARMELLA carrying a box of books.

HARRY: So you're Lennie's wife. Come all the way from Guatemala. That's quite a distance. And here you are teaching English to our kids.

CARMELLA: English is actually the language we spoke at home. My mother teaches American Literature at the University.

CARMELLA puts the books on the table.

HARRY: Thanks for dropping them off. The committee needs to be able to read the book before the meeting but it seems the bookstore is out of copies. People seem to rush towards controversy.

CARMELLA: I hope…the books will be returned in good shape. We only just received them.

HARRY: They will be returned if they are approved.

CARMELLA: It's really just a few parents overreacting. Some of them haven't even read the book and are taking everything out of context.

HARRY: Folks are pretty upset that the board put the book on the list in the first place.

CARMELLA: I put the book on the list.

HARRY: You did?

CARMELLA: I thought the students would appreciate reading a book by an author from where they live. So I suggested the book last year. Principal Jacobs read it, loved it. It went to the board for approval. So it's gone through all the correct steps.

HARRY: You don't find…portions of it…obscene?

CARMELLA: No, I don't. And I'm sure once you've read it you'll agree with—

HARRY: I have read it.

CARMELLA: Well…then I'm sure you can see its literary merits.

HARRY: They say that book by Mr. Lawrence, *Lady Chatterley's Lover*, has its literary merits. Would you like to expose our children to that book, too?

CARMELLA: No. But I would fight for that book to be available in libraries for anyone to read, should they choose.

HARRY: But we are talking about what is being taught in school. To a very impressionable group of young people, including my son.

CARMELLA: So…are you advocating for the book to be removed from the classroom?

HARRY: Yes, I am. I am not just a school trustee, I am an active member of St. Stephen's Church and must represent the concerns of our parishioners.

CARMELLA: Isn't that a conflict?

HARRY: No, in fact, I would say the two align very well. And I would like to remind you...the law states that the duties of a teacher, as defined by the Ontario Education Act, is to teach respect for religion and the principles of Christian morality. We all know that teachers are, generally, more liberal minded and—

CARMELLA: I'm a Christian too, an active member of the Mennonite Church, and I see nothing wrong with this book. In fact, I think it promotes the very best kind of values, showing the triumph of the human spirit, teaching us compassion for others—

HARRY: No need to get excited now.

CARMELA: I'm not excited. ¿Por qué odian la pasión los canadienses?[1]

HARRY: Mrs. Thorpe, I know you mean well, but you're new to Ellice County.

CARMELA: I've been here four years.

HARRY: And you've only been teaching for two. It takes time to understand us, so let me give you a tip. A couple of years teaching doesn't give you much seniority, so tread carefully.

CARMELA: Pardon?

HARRY: Parents are taxpayers and that gets a lot of them to thinking that they're your boss, and if they don't like the way you do things, then....

CARMELA: Then, what? ...they'll fire me?

HARRY: I did not say that. Let me just explain the process here. The Textbook Review committee will meet next week, report to the board—

CARMELA: And who is on the committee?

HARRY: Two trustees, including myself, two teachers, two clergymen and six other taxpayers. We will be reviewing this book plus a few others that have come to our attention.

CARMELA: "A few others" ...Other novels?

HARRY: *Catcher in the Rye* is being reviewed for the second time, *Of Mice and Men* and *The Diviners*.

CARMELA: No. No. That can't be...This is not right. I'm not going to be intimidated by this. I am sure there are many people who will support Peg Dunlop's book, support all these books—

HARRY: Perhaps there are. But due process must take its course. Don't go sticking your neck out too far.

---

1 Why do Canadians hate passion?

Scene Eleven: Fowler Home / Wayford Town Hall

MAYSIE is sweeping the floor. JENNIFER is there.

MAYSIE: What?

JENNIFER: You promised you wouldn't make a big deal about it.

MAYSIE: I didn't have anything do to with it.

JENNIFER: Yeah, right.

MAYSIE: Don't be lippy.

JENNIFER: But you told Mr. Briggs and got him all worked up.

MAYSIE: Harry got himself worked up.

JENNIFER: Well, Kevin says it's your fault.

MAYSIE: Kevin Briggs should mind his own business. Here, take this and finish up. *(MAYSIE hands JENNIFER the broom.)* I need to rake some of those leaves.

JENNIFER: They never ask us what we think. Ever. As if a book is really going to corrupt us.

MAYSIE: When you've done there, the kitchen needs doing.

MAYSIE leaves. JENNIFER takes her coat off and gets to work. After a moment, PEG comes down the stairs. She sees JENNIFER sweeping the floor and stops.

JENNIFER: I'll be done in a minute.

PEG sits on the stairs as JENNIFER sweeps.

I just want you to know that everyone in my class is really mad we can't read your book.

They always say they're preparing us for the real world but they don't want us to know anything *about* the real world.

PEG: Nothing has changed since I was young. They don't like to believe teenagers are thinking persons. Heaven forbid you should know your own mind... or even worse, be a writer.

JENNIFER: I think it's cool.

PEG: If you still want to read *Women of Time*, I can give you a copy.

JENNIFER: I'd like that...but I'm not sure Mum would be very happy. She's weird about what I read.

PEG: Yes, but she's not one of those parents.

JENNIFER: You mean parents who want the book banned?

PEG: I do.

JENNIFER: Yeah. She's not too keen about it. She doesn't want you to know, but she complained to Mrs. Thorpe right off.

PEG: Maysie?

JENNIFER: Now everyone is blaming me that we'll never get to read it.

PEG: Of course you will get to read it. There is no way they can ban a book from high schools, it's been approved, this is all so ridiculous.

JENNIFER: The committee has said all four books should be banned.

PEG: Pardon?

JENNIFER: Kevin Briggs told me. The textbook committee voted to ban the books from all the high schools in Ellice County.

PEG: You're joking.

JENNIFER: Nope.

PEG: The committee just makes a recommendation. The board has the final say. What does the board say?

JENNIFER: Uh…I don't know.

PEG strides over to the bookshelf and looks for books.

PEG: OK….

She starts handing books to JENNIFER.

The Women of Time, Catcher in the Rye, Who Has Seen the Wind, Duddy Kravitz, Lolita. Let's just see if they can stop you from learning about the world.

JENNIFER: I'm not a fast reader. I'll just take one.

PEG: Take them all, give them out to your friends.

MAYSIE: Give out what to her friends?

MAYSIE has entered. She has gardening gloves on.

PEG: Evil, vile literature. Corrupting young minds.

MAYSIE: Jennifer!

PEG: You think I'm writing pornography?

MAYSIE: I didn't know it would go so far. I just didn't want Jennifer reading it. I don't think it's appropriate for her.

PEG: So it's only you Christians that can decide what our children read—

MAYSIE: Not your children, my children.

PEG: You all think you're preaching high morals, but what you're preaching is hatred, authoritarianism, suppressing human thought. Philistines.

MAYSIE: I just don't want Jenny reading your book. It's a small matter.

PEG: Yes, small-minded and mean.

MAYSIE: That's not fair.

PEG: And what exactly is fair? You think I should allow you to work in my house, pay you, while you sneak around and make trouble for me?

MAYSIE: C'mon. If you thought your own kids were getting the short end of the stick, you'd fight for them tooth and nail. That's just—

IRIS (VO): Maysie!

Sound of a crash from upstairs.

MAYSIE: Oh God.

MAYSIE and PEG both rush up. After a moment, MAYSIE comes partway down.

MAYSIE: Call an ambulance. Dial zero. Tell them to come right away.

JENNIFER hurries into the kitchen, MAYSIE runs back up stairs.

HARRY and CARMELLA are back before the audience of concerned parents.

HARRY: This is not an issue of censorship; we are not asking for these four books to be banned, as some are saying. We are only concerned with what books are to be required study by all students in a classroom setting.

CARMELLA: The senior students are ready for books that grapple with the great philosophical questions: the very questions students are asking themselves. Who am I? How do I relate to others? What gives meaning to human experience?

HARRY: Students in a classroom are a captive audience, coming from a wide variety of backgrounds... When a teacher is picking a book to be read by all students, surely they have to keep those differences in mind. They wouldn't pick a book that offends black people or Jewish people...so why do they pick a book that offends our Christian sensibility?

END OF ACT ONE

Catherine Fitch as Peg and JD Nicholson as Harry in the 2016 Blyth Festival production of *If Truth Be Told*.

ACT TWO

Scene Twelve: Fowler Home

PEG is reading letters.

Projection: Handwriting floats above her. "Take your disgusting books and go back west." "Leave our children alone." "Is your aim to destroy the home and family?" "Who do you think you are?"

JENNIFER: Mum says the hospital was awful.

PEG: You'll notice a big difference, she won't wake up much, she may not recognize you...If you are ever here when she has to eat, you'll have to spoon-feed her like a toddler. Well, your mum will show you...I'm afraid it's going to be boring for you.

JENNIFER: I've got reading.

She holds up The Women of Time.

Don't tell Mum.

PEG: Yeah, well, read it while you can. The next thing you know they'll be using them to burn effigies of me.

JENNIFER: Yeah.

PEG: My own mother up there once burned *The Grapes of Wrath* in the woodstove. She'd be horrified about all this, if she knew. It's probably a blessing she doesn't. I've become the kind of woman she'd be ashamed of.

JENNIFER: Sunday the minister said that anyone who didn't sign the petition against the books would have to answer to God. It's like they think we are all going to become devil worshippers if we read certain words. I'm so angry at Mum. If anything, this has made me read more, not less.

PEG: I've been getting the blast from Wayford for years… But I never saw this coming.

JENNIFER: Are you going to stay here?

PEG: I can't leave now. I'm stuck.

JENNIFER: But if you didn't have to, for your mum, would you?

PEG: Ohhh no. I'd be far away. Writing. In a little Paris flat. You thinking of going away to school next year?

JENNIFER: Maybe. I'm not really a school person.

PEG: You should travel, learn, maybe you'll be a writer.

JENNIFER: Maybe.

PEG: First sign of a writer is a reader.

JENNIFER: That'd be…cool.

There is a knock at the door. JENNIFER heads upstairs.

PEG: There's a glass of water with a straw beside the bed. She needs to sit up when she's drinking.

CARMELLA enters.

CARMELLA: Sorry I'm late, we were having auditions for the school play—

PEG: What's the latest from the front lines?

CARMELLA: So…there's going to be a public meeting Tuesday night at the Wayford Hall. The board wants to hear from the community before they convene next week.

PEG: And when the Board meets…they vote?

CARMELLA: They don't have to take the Textbook Review Committee's recommendation. They can overrule that. Harry Briggs is on the board, of course, so that is at least one vote against us. He's speaking on Tuesday, but so am I. We need to make sure we get everyone out who is supportive of the book.

PEG: I don't think I can help.

CARMELLA: I've got calls out to librarians, teachers, newspapers, other writers. We have many allies.

PEG: I can't be seen defending my own book but I feel so useless…

CARMELLA: Are you writing?

PEG: Not much. Between this and Mum.

CARMELLA: How is she?

PEG: Not great. At least she's home now.

CARMELLA: The principal's wife sat in on my English 12 class today. Can you believe it? Along with a trustee. Making sure I don't corrupt any minds.

PEG: What does the principal's wife have to do with it?

CARMELLA: I was so nervous with them watching me, taking notes. I felt like…These people, they…Did you see the paper?

PEG: No…

CARMELLA takes a newspaper out of her bag and shows a full-page ad.

PEG: Who is Renaissance Canada?

CARMELLA: They started the fight against *The Diviners* in Peterborough and now they're supporting other groups.

PEG: Groups? Plural?

CARMELLA: St. Stephen's, the Ellice County Catholic Women's League, something called Parents for Educational Standards. They have money behind them and they are gathering signatures.

PEG: *(Reading.)* "The Voice of the Moderate Majority." Really? A majority?

CARMELLA: I honestly don't think so.

PEG: "...to help defray the costs of fighting book selection policies in the public schools and in support of the Renaissance Crusade for faith, family and freedom..." Crusade?

CARMELLA: I never thought I'd be fighting censorship here. In Canada.

PEG: It's a witch hunt.

Projection: "You may not be the Devil but you are certainly working for him."

Scene Thirteen: Home of Harry Briggs / Wayford Town Hall / Fowler Home

HARRY stands at a table collating three piles of papers, stapling them together, putting them into one pile. MAYSIE watches him.

HARRY: These men may have lost a few battles but they haven't lost the war.

MAYSIE: It's not a war, Harry.

HARRY: It's a battle waged on behalf of our children. Led by these men, Sam Buick, Jim Telford and Renaissance Canada. We're lucky to have their help: working the phones, raising money, galvanizing people. They'll all be here in full force tomorrow night. Wait till you meet them, Maysie.

MAYSIE: I'm just worried things are getting a little out of hand.

HARRY: Have you read these passages?

He gestures to the papers in front of them.

The worst kind of filth. All taken, word for word, from these novels they want to teach our children.

MAYSIE: But just parts. Not the whole books.

HARRY: People don't need to wade into the muck to know that it's dirty. You don't need to drink a whole glass of milk to know that it's sour.

MAYSIE: Harry, where do you get that stuff?

HARRY: *(Annoyed.)* The point being, people will read these excerpts and get a very good idea of what's in these books.

MAYSIE: I don't like what people are saying about Peg Dunlop.

HARRY: Well—

MAYSIE: Or what they're saying about Mrs. Thorpe. That she's a foreigner.

HARRY: People say that kind of thing when they are frustrated. Do you like being called an Uneducated-Redneck-Reactionary-Book-Banning-Bible-Thumper?

MAYSIE: I don't want to be lumped in with one group or another. Neighbours arguing each other. Jennifer furious with me.

HARRY: What are you saying?

MAYSIE: I'm saying… I don't want to be involved in this. I just want to do my job, take care of my kids—

HARRY: Maysie. You're the one who started this. You came to me, remember? Very upset. Feeling like Carmella Thorpe hadn't given you the time of day about your concerns. About what your own daughter was reading. Taking a stand. That was the right thing to do.

MAYSIE: I really don't know about that.

HARRY: And now you have hundreds of people, thousands even, standing with you. Saying, "We agree with you." That is very powerful.

MAYSIE: I didn't ask for all this. I just wanted one book out of the classroom. Not four.

HARRY: *(Gesturing to one of the pages.)* Read this.

> *Projection:"Then they kiss for a long time, his tongue delicately exploring the inside of her mouth. His hands stroking her breasts. She has wanted this, it seems, now, for a long time. He is lying on top of her, and through all their clumsy layers of clothing she can feel his[2]—"*

HARRY: It's from *The Diviners*. Think about young Alistair reading that in a few years...Are you all right with that?

MAYSIE: No.

HARRY: Did you sign the petition?

MAYSIE: Harry, I work for Peg Dunlop. I can't afford to lose my job.

HARRY: You just want to hide in the shadows while other people fight your battles.

---

2 Excerpted from *The Diviners* by Margaret Laurence.

MAYSIE: No, I just—

HARRY: How are folks going to feel when they find out you didn't sign?

MAYSIE: You're going to tell them?

HARRY: No, it won't be me. But these things have a way of getting out. One of the Ladies' Auxiliary decides to go through the lists....Can you hold your head up if that's the case? Are you prepared for that?

MAYSIE: What does the petition say again?

HARRY: *(Reading.)* "We, the undersigned, ask for the immediate removal of the following books from the Ellice County Secondary School curriculum: *The Women of Time* by Peg Dunlop, *The Diviners* by Margaret Laurence, *Catcher in the Rye* by JD Salinger and *Of Mice and Men* by John Steinbeck."

MAYSIE: *Mice and Men*? Didn't we read that in high school?

HARRY: Do you want me to read you a passage from that book?

MAYSIE: No.

HARRY: If you believe your children shouldn't be reading these books, then put your name to it. Be brave about it.

Pause.

We're going to win this, Maysie. We've got hundreds of signatures from across the province—

HARRY turns, and the scene transitions to HARRY and CARMELLA addressing the parents.

HARRY: —supporting our bid to stop the teaching of unsuitable materials in our schools. Teachers are meant to be teaching how to write, math, science, but they get ahead of themselves and think they are meant to influence students' personalities. But what if we don't share the same values?

CARMELA: You must trust teachers to know their students, to know what is appropriate material. Making decisions based on what's best for the whole student body.

HARRY: It is important to note that we taxpayers are paying the salaries of these teachers and should have a say in what they teach.

CARMELLA: A good work of fiction can create parallel worlds that the reader can immerse himself in. Yes, some of the characters may be unsavoury, but students are not going to emulate them, no more than reading about the Second World War will make them become Nazis.

HARRY: The four books being challenged are in contravention of the Education Act on language; banning language which is immoral, vulgar, crude and profane. And so you can see for yourself the kind of language we are talking about here, you can refer to these handouts. *(He holds one up.)*

CARMELLA: One of my favourite books…has a scene of an incestuous rape, a daughter-in-law who disguises herself as a prostitute to trick her father-in-law and a story about adulterous love. And it won't come as a surprise to most of you that the book I am speaking of is the Bible: the most ethical book we have.

HARRY: I want to show you what over three thousand signatures on a petition looks like.

He waves a large pile of papers in the air.

And the boxes behind me? They are filled with hundreds of handwritten letters, from concerned parents and upstanding members of our community. We are not a small, marginal group of crackpots, we are the moderate majority.

CARMELLA: The majority of Canadians support the freedom to read. And we need to come together, as a community: show the country, everyone who is watching this situation very carefully, that we will not tolerate censorship—

HARRY: We need to decide, as a community, what standards we want to set for our children. So I am asking you today—

As the scene continues, MAYSIE comes down the stairs with a load of laundry. She passes the table and notices PEG's writing and stops.

CARMELLA: —to trust that these students are mature, thinking adults who will benefit from reading great works of art. Put pressure on your school trustees—

MAYSIE looks at PEG's writing more closely.

HARRY: —as we decide whether to take the recommendation of the Textbook Review Committee and strike these four books off the reading list in our Secondary Schools.

CARMELLA: —as they decide the future of an open and encompassing education system.

One paper catches MAYSIE's attention. She picks it up and reads.

Projection: Words float above: "Three-year-old boy who drowns. Jumps off high rock into deep water, as family sits around a campfire. Impact on his family."

Sound: For a moment MAYSIE hears the sounds from the evening that Finn died. Splashing in the water as kids jump in the lake, under:

CARMELLA: Words can be very powerful. Transporting us to places that can be difficult. But I would argue that the benefits of reading great literature are huge. I thank you for your support.

HARRY: Will you stand up for our children?

Scene Fourteen: Fowler Home

Nighttime. Sound of rain pouring outside. Someone is rummaging around PEG's desk. Light turns on from upstairs. PEG is coming down the stairs putting on her housecoat. JENNIFER is barefoot, in her nightgown, soaked from the rain.

PEG: What in heaven's name? Jennifer? What's going on?

JENNIFER: Why did you write about my brother?

PEG: What?

JENNIFER: Why'd you write about Finn?

PEG: I was just—

JENNIFER: You going to write him into one of your books?

PEG: I was just exploring an idea. I wasn't really—

JENNIFER: Well, don't, OK?! It's not your story, it's our story!

PEG: Of course it is. My God, you're soaking wet. Stay right there, I'll get a towel.

PEG runs off, coming back a moment later with a towel.

JENNIFER: Mum read it. And now she's going crazy and crying and yelling at me and blaming me.

PEG: OK. OK. I see. Come sit down.

JENNIFER: You're always talking about how badly people treat you. Well maybe it goes both ways. Maybe people don't like your books because you steal stuff and make them dirty.

PEG: C'mon now. I know you're angry but—

JENNIFER: You bet I'm angry. I'm fucking angry.

PEG: No, no, don't talk like that.

JENNIFER: Isn't that the way we country people talk when we get angry? Isn't that what you write in your books?

PEG: I promise I won't write a story about Finn. And I'll speak to your mum, OK? I'll make sure she knows.

JENNIFER: She doesn't like talking about him!

PEG: I know. I'll be careful.

JENNIFER: And now she's mad at me. I never should have told you!

MAYSIE: You're right. You shouldn't have. But it's done now. So come home.

MAYSIE has entered, wet from the rain.

PEG: Maysie, this is just a misunderstanding.

MAYSIE: I wasn't speaking to you. Jennifer.

PEG: C'mon now.

MAYSIE: There's no "misunderstanding."

PEG: I was only making notes. Don't blame Jennifer for telling me.

MAYSIE: Well it's not her place to be yapping about what happened.

JENNIFER: I wasn't yapping! I have a perfect right to talk about my own brother.

MAYSIE: Not to her.

JENNIFER: It's better than you always pretending like he never even existed. There's no pictures anywhere. I'm never supposed to talk about him. She didn't even let me go to the funeral.

MAYSIE: You were too little.

JENNIFER: You never even say his name.

Pause.

Can you not even say his name?!

MAYSIE: Stop it.

Sound: Very softly, building under the following dialogue. MAYSIE hears the sound of the evening that Finn died. Splashing in the water as the kids jump in the lake, sounds around the campfire, building under:

JENNIFER: Dad blames her. She was supposed to be watching him.

PEG: Jennifer.

JENNIFER: Why won't she talk about him? Or even let me talk about him.

PEG: Maysie, I am so sorry about your little boy.

JENNIFER: Would you please just say his name?!

The sound builds to this moment, then is suddenly out. MAYSIE leaves.

PEG: I'll get you some dry clothes and you can go home.

PEG starts to go upstairs.

JENNIFER: Why'd you come back to Wayford anyway? You hate it here, you hate us.

PEG: That's not true. I don't hate Wayford.

JENNIFER: What were you going to write about Finn?

PEG: I wasn't going to—

JENNIFER: You were thinking of something.

PEG: Really, I'm just grasping at straws.

JENNIFER: Just answer me! If you were going to write a story about Finn, how would it go?

PEG: I don't know.

JENNIFER: Would I be in the story?

Pause.

PEG: Finn wouldn't be Finn...he'd be someone else...I suppose I'd try to capture this huge feeling of loss, how quickly life can change...in a heartbeat... because someone looked right instead of left.

JENNIFER: Yeah.

PEG: There's probably a million times your mum saved your lives, from the moment you were born and the one time—

JENNIFER: Would you set it in Georgian Bay?

PEG: I'd probably set it at the quarry over by Clearwater, where the kids swim and the men fish. I know that place fairly well.

JENNIFER: It's deep there. And cold.

PEG: And yes, there might be a sister. An older sister, trying to make sense of what happened. But there being no sense to it. It just happened.

JENNIFER: Yeah, well...what if it almost happens, but it doesn't and the sister stops him at the last minute.

PEG: That would be a different kind of story.

JENNIFER: With a happy ending, because the family would probably stay together.

PEG: And that makes a happy ending? A family staying together?

JENNIFER: Why aren't you with your family?

PEG: It's complicated.

JENNIFER: You think I'm too stupid to get something complicated?

PEG: Our marriage has run its course. Our children have moved on, we found we really don't have that much in common anymore… And Ted doesn't want to move to Wayford. And like it or not, I have to be here.

JENNIFER: He doesn't like Wayford either, huh?

PEG: Maybe you could write the story, how you see it.

JENNIFER: I'm not a writer.

PEG: A writer is a person who writes. That's all. If you write a story with some seriousness, you can be a writer.

JENNIFER: I guess.

PEG: You wouldn't have to show it to anyone, if you don't want to…here take a notebook, I've got lots of empty ones.

PEG gives JENNIFER a notebook.

Don't think about it too much. Just write what you think should happen.

JENNIFER: Maybe I'd have the mom see the boy about to jump, but the sister's closer to him, so she grabs his arm.

PEG: Yes. You could write that. I'd better get you those clothes, before you get a chill.

JENNIFER is lost in thought. PEG goes upstairs. After a moment JENNIFER walks out, with the towel wrapped around her.

Scene Fifteen: Church Meeting Room.

HARRY pulls a chair into the circle and sits.

HARRY: So, well, we didn't get the outcome that we'd all have preferred. The long and the short of it is, the board has voted and their decision is final.

They have decided to put the books back in the hands of our young people, allowing them to remain on curriculum lists. They will be reinstating *Of Mice and Men*, a book filled with profane language. They will be reinstating *Catcher in the Rye*, a book with unsuitable sexual content. They will be reinstating Peg Dunlop's book *The Women of Time* in which two teenagers have relations in the back of a car and an old woman has a obscene liaison with a stranger. It seems we have lost that fight. It seems that teachers' rights have trumped parents' rights, and our rights here, as Christians.

However, we have succeeded on one front. Margaret Laurence's book, *The Diviners*, will not be allowed back in the classroom. The board has supported us on that. So your hard work has still been worthwhile. It is even more worthwhile when you feel the enormous support we've received. The thousands of people who believe in what we are doing. And the encouragement we have received from groups like Renaissance Canada.

I spoke to the folks at Renaissance just before I came here, telling them the outcome of the board meeting, and they encourage us to keep going, build on our momentum. We should not and can not rest easy. We need to be looking at libraries who stock these kind of books. We need to look at government groups like The Canada Council, who give public money, our own tax dollars, to writers like Mrs. Dunlop and Laurence to write these books. And we need to keep the pressure on our school trustees, teachers and principals, continue to let them know what we are watching, that we care deeply about our children, our community and the world we live in.

Scene Sixteen: Fowler Home

CARMELLA has just arrived; she hasn't taken her coat off.

PEG: You won't believe the phone calls I've been getting. Suddenly everyone wants to interview me about it all.

CARMELLA: Yes, you must feel good. Such a vindication.

PEG: But poor Margaret Laurence? Her beautiful book?

CARMELLA: I know. I feel badly about that.

PEG: Shall I put the kettle on?

CARMELLA: No, I won't be able to stay long. I'm directing the school play this year and we have a rehearsal at four.

PEG: You know, I've been thinking. I want to get more involved in these censorship fights. The problem is I tend to want to be liked too much, so I end up retreating, avoiding the whole thing. But now…I think, I could help other writers.

CARMELLA: I am sure…there are groups…they'd be thrilled to have you.

PEG: We could do it together. You speak so well. I could read and—

CARMELLA: Peg. I'm afraid I'm going to have to pull back a little…not be so vocal for a while.

JENNIFER comes out of the kitchen carrying a bowl of applesauce.

JENNIFER: I put the applesauce through the blender so it's really smooth.

CARMELLA: Jennifer.

JENNIFER: Hi, Mrs. Thorpe.

CARMELLA: I didn't know you…

JENNIFER: Yeah.

PEG: Jennifer's been helping me out with Mum. You'd better take that up now. OK? Let me know if you need anything.

JENNIFER goes upstairs. There is an awkward pause.

What do you mean, you have to pull back?

CARMELLA: You know how things are here. People can be…I've just been feeling a bit…

PEG: Oh yes. I know all too well…. Good people who were once kind and friendly suddenly become distant and disappointed. Have you been getting the freeze?

CARMELLA: I didn't want to mention this before but…this whole thing has been very hard on Leonard… and his parents.

PEG: I can imagine. I always worried about the price Mum paid for having me.

CARMELLA: His parents are such lovely gentle people and they've been so understanding but I know their friends have different views.

PEG: Well, when you start teaching *Women of Time*, I'll come in and speak to the class. Properly this time. Get them excited about the book. Read them all the dirty bits.

CARMELLA: Peg…

Pause.

I'm afraid I won't be teaching your beautiful book this year. It's an optional text…we feel we best leave it alone for a while, until things settle down.

You know how much I love it. So it's not that at all. But not all the students are ready. And if we have five or six of the parents requesting that their children have an alternative selection…

PEG: When did you come to this…realization…?

CARMELLA: I had a meeting with my principal and the English Department a couple of days ago, and we came to the conclusion that—

PEG: Oh no. Oh no. They got to you. You've been pressured.

CARMELLA: No, no. It's not like that. The staff have been so supportive. All along the way.

PEG: Is this your decision?

CARMELLA: Ultimately, it's Principal Jacobs' decision. But he and some of the other teachers have expressed a desire for the rest of the school year to run smoothly, without controversy.

PEG: Did he threaten to fire you?

CARMELLA: No.

PEG: Do you want me to speak to him?

CARMELLA: No. No. He didn't threaten me. At all.

PEG: I could do that. I'll stand up for once. Like you've stood up for me.

CARMELLA: No. It's…I wasn't really seeing, when I was in the thick of it…the impact this fight, this important fight, which I am very proud of…but I wasn't really aware the impact it was having on the people around me. And now that I've had time to think, I can see…

that...maybe certain books are just unsuitable for students...not for the same reasons Harry Briggs and his group believe...but perhaps it's actually a disservice to certain books to introduce them to students at this stage in their lives.

PEG: Really??

CARMELLA: I wouldn't call it censorship or anything, but certain books just shouldn't be...now this is a different kind of thing, but think about a book like *To Kill a Mockingbird*. One of my favourite books. But I wouldn't teach it in a school. The number of times the word "nigger" is used...if it was taken out of context...And of course real pornography that is exploitive of women and children—

PEG: How can you even compare the two? Films or photographs of actual women and children in situations that are horribly degrading...absolutely should be stopped, censored, whatever you want to call it...but the printed word? Never.

CARMELLA: I'm sorry. I've upset you. Let's drop it—

PEG: Because it's a slippery slope. Where do you stop? Who decides?

CARMELLA: Yes, but sometimes there are—

PEG: No, not sometimes. You can't believe that, Carmella. Especially not you. Isn't Guatemala...?

CARMELLA: Isn't Guatemala what?

PEG: Don't you think artistic suppression and political suppression go hand in hand?

CARMELLA: This is hardly the same situation as Guatemala. Would you like me to give you a lesson on the political situation there? Would you like to hear about the death squads? Torture? Disappeared journalists and students? You are comparing that with what is happening in Wayford?!

PEG: No, no.

CARMELLA: All I'm saying is it's not all black and white. We have to consider both sides. Is that so crazy?

PEG: You're defending censorship!

CARMELLA: No, I am not! I just…I don't want to be an outsider forever. I like it here. I like these people. They are good, decent people who care about their children. We don't have the same views about books and freedom of expression but…just…one day…I'd like to be an insider. To belong here.

PEG: For me…my art…my writing…my principles… those things are more important than being invited to join bingo night.

CARMELLA: Can't they go hand in hand? Can't we say… let's agree to disagree? Even though I don't share your values, I can still speak to you on the street? Make pies with you at church?

PEG: Believe me, they don't want me making pies with them.

CARMELLA: Oh Peg. I'm just saying I've done my part and I need to stand back a bit. Does that make me a bad person? Haven't I done enough for now?

PEG: Yes, you have done a lot. I know I should be more grateful but…

CARMELLA: Can't you possibly…put all this behind you? Move on?

PEG: No. I can't.

CARMELLA: Can we at least—

JENNIFER appears on the stairs.

JENNIFER: Mrs. Dunlop?

PEG: Yes.

JENNIFER: Something is wrong.

PEG: What kind of something?!

JENNIFER: Your mother. I don't think she's breathing.

PEG hurries up the stairs.

Scene Seventeen: Fowler Home

There are bunches of flowers around the room. JENNIFER and MAYSIE bring in more.

JENNIFER: What should I do with these ones?

MAYSIE: There are no more vases.

JENNIFER: So…?

MAYSIE: Put them in the sink for now.

JENNIFER: Did you tell her those library ladies called?

MAYSIE: Not yet. She's been…well, it's hard losing a mother. So we have to give her some rope, huh?

JENNIFER: Yeah.

MAYSIE: I've got it on my list…There might be some vases up top. Have a look.

JENNIFER heads into the kitchen. PEG comes down from upstairs.

MAYSIE: Were you able to sleep?

PEG: No.

MAYSIE: Can I give you a few messages?

PEG: Can I stop you?

MAYSIE: Reverend Clark needs you to let him know which hymns you've decided on.

PEG: Oh, for God's sake. I thought we talked about that.

MAYSIE: He said you hadn't decided between "Amazing Grace" and "How Great Thou Art."

PEG: I told him I don't care which one. You decide.

MAYSIE: OK. And he wants to know if you're still planning to speak.

PEG: No, I've changed my mind. I can't.

MAYSIE: Then he wondered who you might want to do the eulogy. He said he's happy to but hasn't known Mrs. Fowler for as long as some people.

PEG: Like Harry Briggs?

MAYSIE: Yes. Harry was very good to your mother. He would give a nice speech.... It's just a thought. There's some others. I wrote them down. Maybe upstairs. Give me a minute.

MAYSIE goes upstairs. PEG looks for her cigarettes. JENNIFER appears.

JENNIFER: *(Low.)* I finished your book.

JENNIFER gives PEG back the copy of The Women of Time.

I thought it was good. I really liked it.

PEG: Yeah? What did you like about it?

JENNIFER: The characters and stuff.

PEG: The characters and stuff?

JENNIFER: I liked Lissa and Alphie a lot.

PEG: You weren't corrupted by their sexual fumblings?

JENNIFER: No. But I thought it was sad. They're never going to see each other again and they love each other so much. And the husband and wife are stuck with each other for life and they hate each other.

PEG: Well, life isn't easy.

JENNIFER: No, but…

PEG: You'd prefer a happy ending for everyone?

JENNIFER: Yeah. I think so. Maybe.

MAYSIE can be seen coming down the stairs, but she pauses as:

PEG: Then don't read my books. My books aren't for sissies.

JENNIFER: I'm not a sissy, I just—

PEG: Did you ever write that story we talked about?

JENNIFER: About Finn? No. I don't think I'm a writer.

PEG: Yeah, well, writers have to look at very hard things. It's not a very comfortable life. It's a calling. A horrible, terrible calling. And I don't wish it on anybody. And it certainly doesn't have a god damned happy ending.

MAYSIE comes the rest of the way down.

MAYSIE: Jennifer, can you finish the bathroom for me?

PEG: Run, Jennifer! Get away from the crazy writer lady.

MAYSIE: Stop it. Leave her alone.

PEG: What?

MAYSIE: You act like the whole world's against you.

PEG: Yeah well, right now it feels like that.

MAYSIE: You're so determined to suffer, you can't see right in front of you. Have you seen these flowers? They're all for you.

PEG: Oh no they're not, they're for my mother. Iris Fowler. Pillar of Wayford. Beloved by all.

MAYSIE starts reading the cards on the flowers.

MAYSIE: Look here.... "from your high school friends, Jill and Grace." *(Another card.)* "From all of us at the Ellice County Library," *(Another card.)* "Dear Peg, so sorry for your loss, we love you. Jean and Todd"

PEG: Yes but...

MAYSIE: What? Those people don't count? People who like you don't count? And here, this lovely bunch from Carmella Thorpe, who fought for you tooth and nail. She adores you! Her in-laws, who are Mennonites, came out to that meeting at the hall and sat in the very front row wearing "I support Peg Dunlop" buttons!....Can you not see how so many folks in Wayford support you? That's why they spoke up to their trustees. Wrote letters for you. That's why the other side lost. You can only hear the criticism and none of the praise... Jennifer just told you that she liked your book. And you practically tore her head off.

JENNIFER: I did like it. Really.

MAYSIE: You're right, the whole business went too far. Didn't sit right with me at all. Some people weren't very nice. But that doesn't mean you can't hear the good folks. They're out there. And they're crazy for you.

PEG begins to cry. MAYSIE goes to her and holds her.

That's OK. You cry. You need a good cry. You just lost your Mama and no matter when that happens that's something to cry about....

Pause.

The other day…when I read what you wrote about my boy…I went home and cried. Really cried. I couldn't stop.

PEG: Oh, Maysie… I'm so sorry.

MAYSIE: No. I…that was good. Because I could never cry about him, you know? It's like it happened and everything got stuck inside. And couldn't come out…. My dear sweet little Finnie.

JENNIFER comes in for a hug too.

MAYSIE: Mrs. Fowler was a nice lady. And maybe she wasn't so fond of your books but she was some proud of you. So proud. And that's what you gotta remember. Huh? You gotta hold on to the good stuff. And let the nasty bits go.

HARRY: *(Off.)* Hello? Anyone home?

HARRY comes in from the kitchen carrying a pot. He surveys the scene.

Sorry. Don't mean to interrupt. Laurel's sent some soup over. Turkey noodle. It's still warm.

MAYSIE: That's nice of her, Harry. Mmm, smells good.

MAYSIE takes it into the kitchen.

PEG: Thank you.

HARRY: I'm so sorry, Peg. I was very fond of Iris. She and Mom used to play gin rummy every Thursday night. Did you know that? They'd let me play sometimes.

PEG: No, I didn't know that.

MAYSIE returns.

HARRY: Anyway, I've got to dash. I just wanted to drop that off.

He starts to leave.

PEG: Harry...Would you give the eulogy for Mum?

HARRY: Me?

PEG: Is there another Harry in the room?

Pause.

HARRY: I'd be honoured.

PEG: Good.

MAYSIE: You going home? Can we get a ride that way?

HARRY: Sure. Peg, if there is anything you want me to cover about Iris, let me know. I'll write something up tonight.

PEG: Thank Laurel for me. For the soup.

MAYSIE gets her coat on, hands JENNIFER her coat.

Maysie. I'm going to still need you for a while at least. Is that possible?

MAYSIE: Yup, I'll be back.

PEG: Thank you.

MAYSIE and HARRY leave. JENNIFER pauses.

JENNIFER: So you going to get back to writing now? What are you going to write about?

PEG: I actually have an idea, Jennifer. Finally. It's a good one.

JENNIFER: Is it set in Wayford?

PEG: Oh yes.

JENNIFER: No happy ending, right?

PEG: There's no such thing as happy endings, Jennifer. Something always comes after.

JENNIFER exits, leaving PEG alone. Music rises.

Projection: In cursive:

"Woman writer. Marriage dissolves, returns home.

What does she learn?

Nothing is easy. Nothing is simple."

Then:

"In 2012,

Peg Dunlop of Wayford Ontario,

was awarded the Nobel Prize for Literature."

THE END